ALONZO MOURNING
CENTER OF ATTENTION

BY BILL GUTMAN

MILLBROOK SPORTS WORLD
THE MILLBROOK PRESS
BROOKFIELD, CONNECTICUT

Photographs courtesy of Focus on Sports: cover, pp. 3 (© Jerry
Wachter 1993), 44; NBA Photos: cover inset (Al Messerschmidt),
pp. 29 (Nathaniel S. Butler), 30 (Gregg Forwerck), 35 (Nathaniel S.
Butler), 36 (Richard Lewis), 41 (Barry Gossage), 46 (Scott
Cunningham); Allsport: pp. 4, 17 (Doug Pensinger), 20 (Doug
Pensinger), 26 (Vince Bucci), 33 (Jonathan Daniel), 39 (Jonathan
Daniel), 42 (Jonathan Daniel); Bill Abourjilie, The Virginian Pilot: p.
10; AP/Wide World Photos: pp. 12, 15, 23, 24, 32

Library of Congress Cataloging-in-Publication Data
Gutman, Bill.
Alonzo Mourning : center of attention / by Bill Gutman.
p. cm. — (Millbrook sports world)
Includes bibliographical references and index.
Summary: Describes the life of basketball player Alonzo Mourning,
from his childhood in Virginia through his college years at Georgetown
University to his professional career with the Charlotte Hornets and
the Miami Heat.
ISBN 0-7613-0061-9 (lib. bdg.)
1. Mourning, Alonzo, 1970–   —Juvenile literature. 2. Basketball
players—United States—Biography—Juvenile literature. [1.
Mourning, Alonzo, 1970– . 2. Basketball players. 3. Afro-
Americans—Biography.] I. Title. II. Series.
GV884.M67G88 1997
796.323'092—dc20 [B] [392.1'0947] 96–41785 CIP AC

Published by The Millbrook Press, Inc.
2 Old New Milford Road
Brookfield, Connecticut 06804

ALONZO MOURNING

Alonzo Mourning has probably never had a lazy day in his life. The word "lazy" just isn't in his vocabulary. But never was his incredible work ethic more in evidence than on the night of January 6, 1996. That's when the 6-foot 10-inch (208-centimeter), 245-pound (111-kilogram) center led his Miami Heat teammates onto the floor against the Denver Nuggets.

This wasn't just any game. It was Alonzo's first game back after missing 12 games over a three-week span. He had suffered a partial tear of a tendon in his left foot in a game against Phoenix during the second week in December. The Heat had one of the best records in the National Basketball Association before Alonzo was hurt. But they had lost more than they had won while he was injured.

Alonzo Mourning plays basketball only one way—to win. Here the Miami Heat center works hard for a basket against the Minnesota Timberwolves.

So it was important for the man they call "Zo" to play at an all-star level right away. It wouldn't be easy. Nuggets center Dikembe Mutombo was 7 feet 2 inches (218 centimeters) tall and one of the best defensive players in the league. He had also been a teammate of Zo's at Georgetown University. So the two big men knew each other well.

None of that stopped Zo. He came out hustling at both ends of the court. On offense, he had to work for every hoop. He would muscle his way down low against Mutombo for short hooks and dunks. Or he would go outside and take a jump shot. Coach Pat Riley worked the team's offense around Zo, so he couldn't rest, despite his sore foot.

Finally, the score was tied at 86–86 with 15 seconds left. Once again, the ball went inside to Mourning. He took a quick step and swung past Mutombo for another short hook. Rookie forward Antonio McDyess went up high and appeared to block the shot. But the ball was already on the way down to the hoop. That was goaltending. The basket counted and won the game for the Heat, 88–86.

In his first game back, Alonzo Mourning had scored 38 of his team's 88 points. He also had 10 rebounds while playing 40 of a possible 48 minutes. More important, he had made his team a winner.

"He played great today," said his friend and opponent Mutombo. "He shot the hook very well. I thought I could get more of them, but I was just a hand short."

Zo's Miami teammates were overjoyed that the big man was back on center stage. Guard Bimbo Coles said it best:

"Just his presence gave a lot of guys confidence, including me. It definitely gives us a lot of confidence having him back."

CHILDHOOD PROBLEMS

It would have been very easy for Alonzo Mourning to have taken the wrong road. All the signs were there. Had it not been for his strong character and the right person to show him the way, Zo might not be a top professional athlete today.

Alonzo Harding Mourning, Jr., was born on February 8, 1970, in Chesapeake, Virginia. Chesapeake wasn't far from some of the world's biggest shipyards and military bases. Alonzo Mourning, Sr., worked at one of those shipyards for more than 20 years.

But things weren't always good between Alonzo, Sr., and his wife, Julia. The family lived in Deep Creek, a rural section of Chesapeake. Mr. and Mrs. Mourning did not always get along well, and their home wasn't always a happy one. Alonzo has said that he wasn't abused as a child, but his wasn't an easy home to grow up in.

He played sports with his friends but didn't really think about the future. He was often upset about the situation at home. Then, in 1980, his parents finally separated. Alonzo was only 10 years old then, and for a while there was a question about just where he would live. He wound up in a group home for a time as his parents planned to divorce.

"I was like any other kid then," he said. "Rebellious. I wasn't pleased with the situation when my parents planned to divorce and I didn't want to go through a custody battle."

It was then that Alonzo found the person who would change his life. In a way it was pure luck. Alonzo called it a "gift from God."

The woman's name was Fannie Threet. Alonzo had met her while he was in elementary school and she was a substitute teacher. What he didn't know then was that Fannie Threet often took troubled children into her home and gave them the love and security they couldn't find elsewhere. At that time, she had two of her own children and five foster children in her home.

When she saw that Alonzo desperately needed a home, she brought him to live with her.

"He [Alonzo] just took to Mom and he never wanted to leave," said Robert "Bud" Threet, one of Fannie's two biological children. "Mom has a way of making people feel at home."

Being at Fannie Threet's home gave Alonzo stability. He knew he was loved and wanted, and never got in trouble on the streets. Mrs. Threet said that he never caused her any problems.

"He was always very obedient, very mannerly," she said. "There might have been only one time when I had to speak to him harshly. He was so big that he once lifted one of the other boys up in the air and I had to run out and order him to put the boy down. He did, and that was that."

As for Alonzo, he credits Fannie Threet with helping him to get his act together.

"She used to tell me I didn't have to be angry and fight the whole world," he has said.

As it turned out, Alonzo's biological parents got together again and in 1981 had a second child, his sister Tamara. But Alonzo continued to live with Fannie Threet. His parents separated again in 1982 and were divorced in September 1983.

By that time, Alonzo had begun to discover something else—the sport of basketball.

BASKETBALL BEGINNINGS

When Alonzo came to live with Fannie Threet, he was already nearly 6 feet (183 centimeters) tall and wore a size 12 shoe. He and Bud Threet began going down the block where the kids had built tree houses and put up a rough basketball court.

"It was a homemade hoop and backboard just nailed to a tree," said Bud Threet. "But Al [Alonzo] liked all the sports at that point. It was football one day, kickball the next. Like any kid growing up."

Then came the 1982 collegiate national championship basketball game between Georgetown University and the University of North Carolina. Alonzo sat in front of a television set that night and watched Georgetown's freshman center, Patrick Ewing, swat away the first four Carolina shots. All four were called goaltending, and the baskets counted. But young Alonzo was impressed by Ewing's performance.

Shortly after that, Zo began to concentrate more on basketball. Since he was already taller than most boys his age, he usually played center, like Ewing. And he could always block shots. Playing for an Amateur Athletic Union (AAU) team, he blocked an amazing 27 shots in one game.

Alonzo kept growing. By the time he was in the eighth grade he was 6 feet 4 inches (193 centimeters) tall. He was so good that he was already playing on the Indian River High School junior varsity. His teammates were all ninth and tenth graders.

"He was the youngest guy on the team but the tallest," said JV Coach Freddie Spellman. "And he was the same type of player as he is today—aggressive defensively, always very intense. But he was quiet."

He was also becoming a better player. Fannie Threet took him to see an old friend, the basketball coach at Old Dominion University. He, too, saw Alonzo's

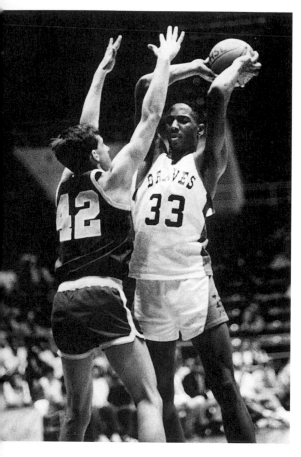

As a senior at Indian River High in 1987, Zo (33) was a dominating player and one of the top college prospects in the country.

potential and made it possible for him to attend basketball camps during the summer. When Zo entered Indian River High in the fall of 1984, he was getting close to his full height of 6 feet 10 inches.

Alonzo's work ethic was already developed. He worked hard on the basketball court and at his schoolwork. When he was old enough, he held a job after school. There were times when schoolwork didn't come easy, but he wouldn't quit on that, either. He knew he would have to do well in school in order to go to college.

By the time he was a junior, he was simply the best player on the team. Playing under Coach Bill Lassiter, Alonzo led Indian River to an unbeaten season and the state championship. Along the way he became Virginia's High School Player of the Year. As good as he was becoming, he never let it go to his head. Fannie Threet was partly responsible for that.

"She always put me in my place, kept me down to earth, and pulled my head out of the clouds," Alonzo said.

The librarian at Indian River High, Sandy Mills, remembered Alonzo as a kid who handled his basketball success in high school very well.

"He didn't think he was better than anybody else and was never disrespectful," Ms. Mills said. "He really was a very sweet kid."

As a senior in 1987–1988, Alonzo was even better. In fact, Bob Gibbons, who specialized in ranking high school players, called Alonzo the top player in the country and the best collegiate prospect among seniors. College recruiters began coming in droves to see him play.

He began going on recruiting trips to visit colleges, and also continued to play outstanding ball with his team. Through it all, he still managed to follow Fannie Threet's number one rule. Homework gets finished first. Alonzo's teachers said his work was always in on time.

Because he knew he had to have a certain score on his Scholastic Aptitude Test (SAT) in order to be eligible to play college ball his first year, he worked hard once again. He spent hours with a tutor in the school library and got the score he needed with plenty of room to spare.

He finished his senior year at Indian River as the team's leading scorer and rebounder. But better yet, Alonzo Mourning was then named the National High School Player of the Year by both Gatorade and *USA Today*. And his high school yearbook named him the most likely to succeed.

He sure had a lot to live up to.

HOYA FRESHMAN STAR

Though he had visited a number of colleges, Alonzo began to lean toward Georgetown University in Washington, D.C. He had followed Patrick Ewing's career there ever since that NCAA title game in 1982. With Ewing at center, the Hoyas had won one national championship and had reached the title game two other times.

He also felt that Coach John Thompson ran a fine program. The coach cared deeply about his players and stressed education. More than 95 percent of Thompson's players had earned their degrees, including Ewing.

To top it off, Thompson was a former 6-foot 10-inch (208-centimeter) center who had been an All-American at Providence College and had played in the NBA with the Boston Celtics. There, he was a backup center to the great Bill Russell. So Thompson was just the right coach for big men. Alonzo also liked the Hoyas' aggressive style of play, especially at the defensive end. It seemed like the perfect fit for him.

In the fall of 1988, Alonzo traveled to Washington to begin his studies and his college basketball career at Georgetown. Though he was 2 inches (5 centimeters) shorter than Patrick Ewing, Alonzo knew that he would be compared with his predecessor, who had gone on to star with the New York Knicks of the NBA.

Under Coach Thompson, the Hoyas did not have a star system. Their offense wasn't geared to one player being the big scorer. Ewing, for instance, averaged more points in the pros than he ever had at Georgetown. But Alonzo had always been a team player. Being a superstar and hogging the spotlight wasn't his game. Winning was.

The Georgetown team from 1988 to 1990 was a good one. Besides Alonzo, Charles Smith and Mark Tillmon were both reliable scorers. Coach Thompson also shuttled players in and out very often. He wanted to keep fresh legs on the court so the Hoyas could play their aggressive, pressing defense.

Not surprisingly, Alonzo won the starting job at center. His aggressive, almost combative attitude fit right in with the team's philosophy. He hit the

Early in his freshman year at Georgetown, Zo began making a name for himself. He could dunk over anyone and in just his third varsity game blocked an amazing 11 shots.

boards hard, was an outstanding shot blocker, and on offense could score from in close. In his third varsity game, Zo attracted national attention. The Hoyas defeated St. Leo University, 95–62. And the freshman center showed his skills by blocking an amazing 11 shots!

Alonzo had to make many adjustments as a freshman. He had become the starting center on one of the best college teams in the country. He had to balance basketball with his studies. At the same time, he had to adjust to being a celebrity.

The basketball part was close to perfect. The Hoyas finished the regular season with a 22–4 record, winning the Big East Conference. When they topped Boston College, Pittsburgh, and Syracuse to win the Big East Tournament, the team was ranked second in the nation. They were then the top seed in the East Region of the NCAA tournament. Many felt that the Hoyas had a shot at the national championship.

Georgetown won three more games before losing to Duke in the Regional Final, 85–77. They had been just one step away from the Final Four. But not even the loss could take away the great freshman season that Alonzo had produced.

In 34 games, the big freshman averaged 13.4 points and 7.3 rebounds a game. Those are relatively modest numbers. But he also led the nation with 169 blocked shots and had an outstanding 60.3 shooting percentage from the field.

After the season, Alonzo was named to the Big East All-Rookie team and second team All Big East. He was also chosen the Big East's Defensive Player of the Year.

Alonzo led the Hoyas into the NCAA Tournament his freshman year. Here he blocks a shot in a regional game against North Carolina State. He was already one of the top college shot blockers in the nation.

"Mourning has already shown himself to be a talented, big-game player," one reporter wrote. "He does many of the same things Patrick Ewing did [at Georgetown] and has the potential to follow Ewing as a great pro player."

For Alonzo Mourning, everything seemed to be coming up roses. What he didn't know then was that perhaps the two most trying years of his life lay ahead.

A CENTER AT POWER FORWARD

Prior to his sophomore season of 1989–1990, many predicted that Alonzo would be an All-American center by the end of the year. But before basketball even began, Coach Thompson was concerned that his young star wasn't paying enough attention to his studies. One day, he sat Alonzo down and made his point.

The coach asked Alonzo to picture himself as the most dominant force in the NBA, a superb player who thought of little else but his sport.

"What if you found out then—and only then—that you had a mind?" the coach asked. "That God had also given you—and only you—the gift to cure cancer. Would that bother you?"

Coach Thompson had made his point. Alonzo realized that he had to develop himself in all areas, and after that his grades always remained good. He explained part of the reason:

"I cut down on the parties after that," he admitted. "That was part of keeping things in perspective. There will always be parties. Now I had other priorities."

Once the season started, there was something else for Alonzo to handle. The Hoyas had a substitute center the year before named Dikembe Mutombo. He was from Africa and hadn't played much basketball before he came to Georgetown. But in the 1989–1990 season he began improving rapidly. He was also 7 feet 2 inches (218 centimeters) tall, 4 inches (10 centimeters) taller than

Alonzo. Coach Thompson began to feel that the team would be strongest with Mutombo playing at center and Alonzo moving to power forward.

It was not an easy transition for Alonzo. A center usually plays with his back to the basket on offense. A forward usually faces the basket. Offensive moves are different. But some felt that the change would help Alonzo. He would become a better passer and learn to drive to the basket, skills that would prepare him for a professional career.

At first, the lineup change seemed to be working. Mutombo wasn't the offensive player that Alonzo was, but his rebounding and shot blocking were outstanding. Alonzo was playing well, also. The team won its first 14 games, but then began to struggle a bit. They lost five late-season Big East games. Then they were beaten in the second round of the Big East tournament and the second round of the NCAA Tournament. The Hoyas' final record was 24–7.

Most of Alonzo's numbers were up from his freshman year. He started all 31 games and averaged 16.5 points and 8.5 rebounds. Mutombo led the team with 10.5

Zo's tough style of play resulted in his being fouled often. His total concentration could even be seen on the free-throw line, where he became a fine foul shooter.

caroms a game. The big change was in blocked shots. After swatting away 169 as a freshman, Zo blocked just 69 as a sophomore. That's because Mutombo was in the middle and getting most of the chances to reject the ball.

Despite his change of position, Alonzo was named Co-Defensive Player of the Year in the Big East and a first team All-Big East selection. He had also decided to major in sociology and indicated that his goal was to get his degree with his class on time.

But the 1990–1991 season would be different. Mutombo was back for one more year at center, and Zo was once again the starting power forward. He was still a highly competitive and aggressive player. At times the Hoyas would go into a full-court press and Coach Thompson would leave Mutombo in but bring Alonzo to the bench. That was really tough for Zo to take.

Then came the fourth game of the season. The Hoyas were playing an outstanding Duke team, which was led by their 6-foot 11-inch (211-centimeter) All-American forward, Christian Laettner. Zo was playing Laettner straight up and totally dominating the Blue Devil star. Midway through the second half, Zo already had 22 points and 10 rebounds, while Laettner had just 14 points on 5-for-22 shooting.

But after a scramble under the boards, Alonzo limped off the court. Without Zo, Duke went on to win the game, 79–74. But the real bad news was that Alonzo had a strained arch in his left foot, the first injury of his career. He would miss the next nine games, and it all but killed his season.

Even after he returned, both his play and the play of the Hoyas were inconsistent. The team lost five of its last six regular-season games, lost in the Big East Tournament, and finally lost to the University of Nevada at Las Vegas (UNLV) in the second round of the West Regional of the NCAA Tournament. That gave the Hoyas a 19–13 record for the year.

As for Alonzo, he played in just 23 games, averaging 15.8 points and just 7.7 rebounds. He blocked only 55 shots. The word was that he was unhappy playing power forward. He received no postseason honors after the 1990–1991 season. Suddenly, the great promise he had shown as a freshman had disappeared. The question was, what would happen in his senior year?

A GREAT COMEBACK

Before Alonzo returned to Georgetown for his senior year in 1991–1992, there were some rumors that he might leave school and enter the NBA draft early. Zo stopped those rumors in a unique way. He talked about something other than basketball.

"My foster mother [Fannie Threet] has never seen me play once," he explained. "But nothing will stop her from coming to my graduation."

It was a sound decision and one that was well thought out. Even Coach Thompson knew Zo would be back. "When I asked him last spring what he was going to do, stay or leave, he said he thought he needed to mature some more," the coach explained. "I told him I thought he was correct. End of story."

For the first time, Zo did not play organized basketball in the summer. He worked out regularly with current and former Georgetown players, including Ewing and Mutombo. And he also helped answer constituent mail for United States Representative Thomas Bliley of Virginia. When he returned to Georgetown he was hungry and eager to play.

"I feel like a volcano ready to erupt," he said.

With Mutombo having graduated, Alonzo would be back at center for the first time since his freshman year. Coach Thompson felt that he would pick up right where he left off.

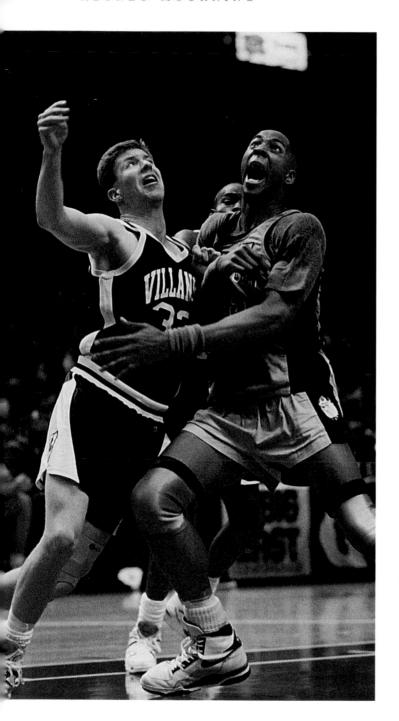

"Last year Zo would have gotten all the blocked shots and rebounds Dikembe got if I had put Zo at center."

Alonzo also said he would make a big effort to curb some of the hostility he often showed on the court. In the past, he was often involved in pushing, shoving, and trash talking. Some felt he was too combative and that it would hurt him.

"You can't take the emotion out of a player," he said, "and emotion has been with me since I played my first organized game in seventh grade. But I'm trying to control it. I look at things with more of an eye to how they'll affect me in the long run. Is it going to stain my image or disrupt me mentally or physically?

Back at center his senior year, Zo treated every game like a war. Here he battles for position underneath against Big East rival Villanova.

"My freshman year I definitely didn't think that way. Now I say to myself, 'Hey, that's not the road to go.'"

Once Zo was back at center, it was as if he had returned home. In the first two games of the season he had a total of 56 points, 24 rebounds, and 14 blocked shots. Two games later, against Delaware State, he grabbed 22 rebounds and swatted away 9 shots. In the Hoyas' first Big East game against Villanova, the big center had 24 points, 15 rebounds, and 8 blocks. He was playing the best basketball of his life.

Unfortunately, the Hoyas' supporting cast wasn't as good as in past years. Yet Alonzo gave 100 percent each minute he was on the court. One of his biggest assets was keeping blocked shots in play. Some shot blockers just swat the ball away, often out of bounds, giving it back to the offensive team. When Zo blocked a shot, he tried to tap it to a teammate at the same time.

In a game against Boston College in February, Alonzo showed how superior he had become. The game went into double overtime with the Hoyas dropping an 88–86 decision. Despite the loss, Alonzo was the game's most dominant player. He scored 38 points, grabbed 16 rebounds, and blocked 6 shots. He impressed everyone, including B.C.'s tough center, Bill Curley, and the coach, Jim O'Brien.

"He [Alonzo] gets up so high so quickly that he could probably catch some of those shots he blocks," Curley said. "It's as if someone is throwing him a lob. He can just tap the ball out to a teammate, like an outlet pass."

Coach O'Brien described Zo this way: "Alonzo has gotten away from that chippiness he once had. If O'Neal doesn't come out, I can't believe Alonzo won't go number one, Laettner included. And I think Laettner is a great player."

O'Brien was referring to the NBA draft and to Shaquille O'Neal of Louisiana State University, a 7-foot 1-inch (216-centimeter) center considered an excellent pro prospect. Like others, O'Brien rated Zo right behind O'Neal.

But there was still a season to finish. The Big East allowed six fouls before disqualification that year, and the games were very rough. To show the kind of pounding that Alonzo had to take under the basket, he became the most fouled college player in the country. Players were always pushing, pulling, slapping, and hacking him. But he also played a physical game and got payback for the fouls by sinking more than 75 percent of his free throws.

He had some other fine games, scoring 24 against Villanova, with 15 rebounds and 8 blocks. In a win over Providence he had 28 points and 12 boards. His numbers against the University of Miami included 26 points and 7 blocks. He had surely reclaimed his position as one of the top players in the land.

Once again the Hoyas went no farther than the second round of the NCAA Tournament, this time eliminated by Florida State University. So Alonzo had never reached a Final Four. Georgetown had just a 22–10 record in 1991–1992. That was disappointing. But as an individual, big Zo had made a remarkable comeback from the season before.

In 32 games, he averaged 21.3 points and 10.7 rebounds. His 160 blocks were second best in the nation. He also hit 59.5 percent of his shots from the field and 75.8 percent from the free-throw line—solid stats. In addition, he finished his Hoya career as the school's fourth-highest career scorer and third-best rebounder. His 453 career blocks placed Zo second only to Patrick Ewing, and his average of 3.77 blocks a game was the best in school history.

Better yet, after the season he was named a first team All-American by the Associated Press, was Big East Defensive Player of the Year, Eastern Basketball Player of the Year, and a finalist for the prestigious Wooden and Naismith awards, both of which were won by Duke's Christian Laettner. But when the Henry Iba Defensive Player of the Year award was presented, the winner was Alonzo Mourning!

Alonzo had one more world to conquer at Georgetown. In the spring of 1992, he proudly accepted his degree in sociology as Fannie Threet and many of his friends looked on. In his four years at Georgetown, Alonzo had weathered the storm and come out a winner.

ROOKIE NBA CENTER

There was no doubt that Zo would be one of the first picks in the NBA draft. When Shaquille O'Neal announced that he was turning pro, he rose to the top of the class. The Shaq became the league's number one pick and was taken by the Orlando Magic. The next selection belonged to the Charlotte Hornets. The team wasted no time in making Zo the number two pick.

The Hornets were an NBA expansion team that had started play in the 1987–1988 season. Like most new teams, the first few years were difficult. The Hornets lost many more games than they won.

Then in 1991, the team drafted power forward Larry Johnson from Nevada–Las Vegas. Johnson stepped in to average 19.2

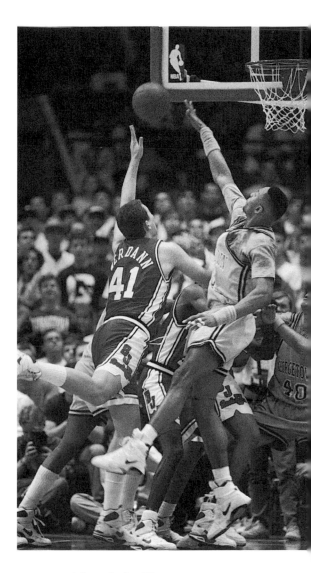

Though the Hoyas never won a national title during Zo's years, he played hard to the end. Here he blocks a shot by Robert Werdann of St. John's during a Big East semifinal game his senior year.

NBA Commissioner David Stern congratulates Alonzo after the Charlotte Hornets made him the second pick in the 1992 NBA draft, right behind Shaquille O'Neal, who went to the Orlando Magic.

points and 11 rebounds a game. The budding superstar was the NBA Rookie of the Year.

But even with Johnson in the lineup, the Hornets were just 31–51 for the year. Now, however, they had Zo to go with "LJ," hoping that their new one-two superstar combination would make them a winner.

Though he had not played a single game as a pro, Alonzo held out during the entire preseason before agreeing to a contract. He finally signed a multiyear, multimillion-dollar pact and joined his new teammates for the start of the 1992–1993 season.

Zo knew that playing center in the NBA wouldn't be easy. There were some great centers already in the league. Hakeem Olajuwon of the Houston Rockets, Patrick Ewing of the New York Knicks, and David Robinson of the San Antonio Spurs were all superstars. Dikembe Mutombo, Alonzo's former teammate at Georgetown, had become an outstanding center with the Denver Nuggets. And big Shaquille O'Neal was coming into the league with Zo.

Those centers were all 7 feet (213 centimeters) or taller. Zo was 6 feet 10 inches, and would be giving up 2 to 4 inches (5 to 10 centimeters) whenever he went up against the other top pivotmen. But he made up for his lack of height with physical strength, drive, and a tremendous will to win. Once on the court, he more than earned his money with a huge effort every night.

While Shaquille O'Neal was living up to his notices and getting all kinds of publicity, Zo was quietly showing everyone that he was a force to be reckoned with as well. Like Ewing before him, he was proving to be a better scorer in the pros than he had been at Georgetown. And he was still a fine rebounder and shot blocker. One of his biggest boosters early in the season was the Phoenix Suns' Charles Barkley, one of the league's top players.

"Alonzo Mourning is going to be the next great, great, unbelievable player," said Barkley.

With two top rookie centers coming into the league the same year, there was talk of a long-term rivalry. In the eyes of some, O'Neal versus Mourning would be to the 1990s what former greats Wilt Chamberlain versus Bill Russell had been to the 1960s.

"I think people see a reincarnation of Chamberlain and Russell," said Orlando Magic general manager Pat Williams. "[Shaq's] power, size, and brute

strength against Mourning's quickness, agility, and hostility. The far bigger player, the true Goliath, being combated by the smaller, more agile, maybe more athletic center."

But Zo didn't like that kind of hype. His game was to play hard against everybody, not just for his matchups with Shaq.

"I'm not hyping up some rivalry," he told the press. "That's your little game, trying to create this rivalry. I'm not into that. You guys cooked this whole thing up, but I don't get excited by it at all."

Alonzo continued to play hard against everyone. Fitting in alongside Larry Johnson and the rest of his new teammates, Zo helped the Hornets become winners with a 44–38 record. The team also made the playoffs for the first time in its history.

Zo's numbers were impressive. In 78 games he scored 1,639 points for a 21 average. He also grabbed 805 rebounds, 10.3 a game. His 271 blocked shots were fourth best in the league behind Olajuwon, O'Neal, and Mutombo. Shaquille O'Neal was Rookie of the Year, but Zo wasn't far behind.

In the first round of the playoffs the Hornets surprised the Boston Celtics, eliminating them in four games, 3–1. But then going against Patrick Ewing and a very good Knicks team the young Hornets showed their inexperience, losing in five, 4–1. But Zo had led the Hornets in both scoring and rebounding. In nine playoff games he averaged 23.8 points and 10 rebounds.

Shaquille O'Neal might have gotten most of the attention, but there was little doubt that Alonzo Mourning had also arrived.

As an NBA rookie, Zo played the same aggressive, nonstop game that had been his trademark at Georgetown. Here he slams one home against the Los Angeles Lakers.

NBA STAR

At the beginning of the 1993–1994 season, most NBA people felt that Shaquille O'Neal had taken his place beside the big three—Olajuwon, Ewing, and Robinson. There were now four elite centers in the league. Zo was considered just a notch behind. Maybe it was because he was a few inches shorter. He had to prove himself that much more.

Dikembe Mutombo had become a fine defensive center, but wasn't much of a scorer. Zo, however, could do it at both ends of the court. There was little doubt that he was very close to being on a par with the other four. But he still paid little attention to that kind of comparison.

He had remained close friends with the other Georgetown alumni, Ewing and Mutombo. Yet he played them as hard as anyone. To Zo, every game was the equivalent of a war.

"The bottom line is about wanting to be the best," he said. "I'm motivated by any player who tries to keep me from doing what I want."

But the Hornets' plans hit a snag right away when Larry Johnson suffered a herniated disk in his back prior to the start of the season. When he began to play, he was at less than full strength. Then he suffered a lower back strain that would cause him to miss 31 straight games. LJ wouldn't be the same dominant player until the final weeks of the season.

That put more of the burden on Alonzo's broad shoulders. By December, he was playing outstanding basketball. In a game against the Celtics, he swept the

Although Alonzo and fellow Georgetown alumnus Patrick Ewing are good friends off the court, they always play very hard against each other. In this game against the Knicks, Zo shoots a jumper over the outstretched arm of Ewing.

boards to the tune of 18 rebounds. Later, he had two straight games in which he scored 36 points. He averaged 23.9 points and 10.2 rebounds for the month.

But then he sprained an ankle and missed six games, returning on January 11. Against the Lakers on January 14, he had 11 offensive rebounds. In another game, he intimidated the Miami Heat by blocking 8 shots. Later in the month Zo was named to the Eastern Conference All-Star team as a reserve. It was to be his first All-Star Game.

But once again the injury jinx struck. This time he tore a muscle in his left calf and was out from January 28 to March 8, missing 16 more games. In the 22

The worst thing for an NBA player is not to play. In 1993–1994 both Zo (left) and fellow Hornet star Larry Johnson were injured at the same time. They continued to stay with the team, but sitting on the bench in street clothes was not what either wanted to do.

total games he missed prior to his return, the Hornets were 6–16. With both Zo and Larry Johnson back for the final weeks the team came on to finish at 41–41 for the season, missing the playoffs by a single game.

In 60 games, Zo averaged 21.5 points and 10.2 rebounds, very consistent with his rookie year. His 188 blocks for a 3.13 average was fourth in the league behind Mutombo, Olajuwon, and Robinson. He had more than Ewing and O'Neal. Only the injuries prevented him from having a super season.

Off the court, Alonzo was also becoming a superstar, but for a very different reason. Like most top players, he had several endorsement deals and did some commercials. It's another way for top players to make big bucks today. But he still found time to give back.

He had an especially soft spot for children. One reason was his own childhood and what Fannie Threet had done for him by taking him into her home.

"I've learned how much she meant to my development," Zo said. "My own situation was that I had the right people around me. A lot of children aren't that fortunate. Kids are like sponges. You can affect how they think."

For that reason, Alonzo began spending as much time as he could at the Thompson Children's Home in Charlotte. The home is for neglected and abused children. There are usually about 40 at a time, between the ages of 5 and 11. The children are given love and therapy before being placed in foster homes. And Alonzo has helped tremendously.

"Primarily, he's just a friend," said Tom Haselden, the director of development at the facility. "But he's a natural. It's amazing to see him out playing basketball with boys who idolize him, but it's even more amazing to see him in the cottages talking to little girls—who have no idea who he is—about pigtails and dolls. He treats the children 100 percent like human beings."

In 1994, Zo joined a group of NBA players who toured the People's Republic of China. Here Zo (right) and fellow NBA star Penny Hardaway of Orlando, have fun with their Chinese tour guide as they visit the historic Great Wall of China.

Zo once showed up for a Valentine's Day party wearing a tiny party hat and passing out balloons. So much for his image as one of the bad boys of the NBA. When a seven-year-old girl named Melissa was asked about Alonzo, she quickly replied, "He's perfect."

HORNET CHALLENGE

In the 1994–1995 season, it looked as if the Hornets were coming of age. Both Mourning and Johnson were healthy, and had fine support from guards Muggsy Bogues and Hersey Hawkins, sixth man Del Curry, and veteran backup center

Robert Parrish. It was apparent from the beginning that the team was on its way to its best season ever.

Led by Alonzo and LJ, the Hornets finished the season with a 50–32 record. They were two games behind the Indiana Pacers in the Central Division and had the eighth-best record in the league. The Hornets were still not considered one of the league's elite, but some observers felt they were getting close.

In Mourning and Johnson, the club had outstanding young players at center and power forward. Bogues, just 5 feet 4 inches (163 centimeters) tall, was quick and deceptive, a fine point guard despite his small size. Hawkins could be a deadly shooter at the off-guard position, and Curry could really light it up off the bench. The consensus was that the team was a player or two away from competing with the best the league had to offer.

In his third season, Zo continued to be amazingly consistent. He played in 77 games, averaging 21.3 points, 14th best in the league. His rebounds were down slightly to 9.9 per game, but he was the fifth-best shot blocker at 2.92 per contest. He still

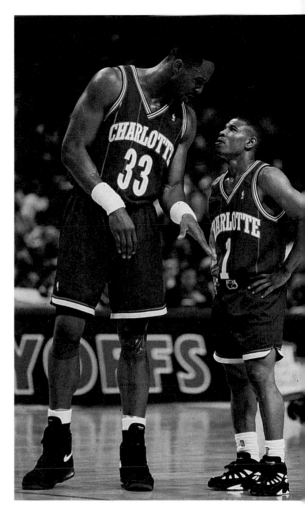

It was quite a contrast when Zo and Hornet point guard Muggsy Bogues, the NBA's smallest player, stood together on the court.

played every game like it was a war, and some criticized him for his demeanor. He often seemed belligerent, ready for a fight, and with a continual scowl on his face.

"When people see my facial expressions, they think I'm mad at somebody," Zo said, "but a lot of times I'm just disappointed at something I've done wrong out there. I'm not an angry guy. I'm not a bad guy. But I'm not the kind of guy who can play with a smile on his face."

The bottom line was that Zo was a competitor. He was well paid to be a professional basketball player, and he always gave his team a complete effort. Now he hoped to help take the Hornets deeper into the playoffs. But in the first round the team had to meet the Chicago Bulls in a best-of-five series. The Bulls had gotten a big boost late in the season when their all-time great superstar, Michael Jordan, came out of a brief retirement to rejoin the team.

The series was considered a toss-up. The Bulls didn't have the strength underneath to match Zo and LJ. But the Hornets, on the other hand, lacked all-around players like Jordan and Scottie Pippen. In addition, the Bulls had won three NBA titles prior to Jordan's retirement. The team had playoff experience.

And that experience might have been the difference. The Bulls took the first game in overtime, 108–100. Then in game two, Zo showed how dominant he could be. He scored 23 points and grabbed 20 rebounds as the Hornets evened the series with a 106–89 victory. But it would be a last hurrah. The Bulls won the third game, 103–80, as the Hornets played poorly. Zo had just 13 points and 7 rebounds. Chicago then wrapped it up with an 85–84 win in the fourth game, eliminating the Hornets from the playoffs.

In four playoff games, Zo averaged 22 points and 13.2 boards, good numbers. But he was bitterly disappointed by the loss. As always, he had played his heart out. His coach at Charlotte, Allan Bristow, said it had been that way for three years.

"Zo never has to be told when to work," the coach said. "I don't think I've ever seen anyone with his kind of discipline right out of college. He's very serious about his profession."

But just when it looked as if the Hornets were on the brink of becoming a top team, there was an unexpected turn of events. And Alonzo Mourning was right in the middle.

A SHOCKING TRADE AND A NEW TEAM

Alonzo's original contract was up following the 1994–1995 season. During that time, huge sums of money were being paid to top NBA rookies and to the league's superstars. In fact, just two years earlier, Larry Johnson had signed a mind-boggling, 12-year deal worth some $84 million. That contract might have set a new standard for the league.

Now the Hornets wanted to try to sign their talented center to a long-term contract. But as the 1995–1996 season neared, Zo still wasn't signed, even though the numbers that were coming out of Charlotte seemed huge to the average person.

Zo played well against the Chicago Bulls in the 1994–1995 playoffs, showing his speed by going around Toni Kukoc for a slam. But it wasn't enough as the Hornets lost the series, 3–1.

It was learned that the Hornets' final offer to Zo was a seven-year contract worth slightly more than $78 million. Most people couldn't believe it when Alonzo said no. It wasn't enough. He felt that in the present NBA market, he could get an even better deal.

"I want to get as much as I can out of this game," he said. "If people want to criticize me for that, then I can't convince them otherwise."

The Hornets had no choice. They didn't want to let Alonzo walk away as a free agent. Just before the start of the season, they shocked the basketball world by trading Zo to the Miami Heat, getting star forward Glen Rice in return. Though he knew it might happen, it wasn't easy for Zo to leave Charlotte.

Prior to the 1995–1996 season, the basketball world was shocked when the Hornets traded Alonzo to the Miami Heat. At a press conference, Miami coach Pat Riley introduces Zo to the Miami media.

"I didn't think I would ever leave Charlotte," he said. "I thought I was going to spend the rest of my career there, start a family there. . . . But it's all about getting what you deserve based on what the market is. I've worked hard to get myself in the position I'm in. I'm trying to prosper and enjoy the fruits of my labor.

"I apologize to the people of Charlotte, and I want to thank them dearly for their support over the years. I'm sorry things turned out the way they turned out."

Most of Zo's teammates at Charlotte understood what had happened. Veteran Robert Parrish echoed the feeling of the team.

"That's the way negotiations go sometimes," Parrish said. "Everybody respects Alonzo's decision. We don't particularly like it, but we respect it."

People outside of basketball were also sorry to see him go. Louise Rice, the director of volunteer services at the Thompson Children's Home, knew that they were losing a valuable asset.

"That's business," she said. "But we're talking about the personal side of Zo. He cared a lot about the kids. We'll miss him."

The personal side of Alonzo Mourning was something a lot of people didn't know much about. He rarely talked about the things he did away from the basketball court. But he was more than just a greedy athlete who wanted all the money he could get for himself.

Two years earlier it was Alonzo who had helped his former high school coach, Bill Lassiter, find a new heart when Lassiter needed a heart transplant to save his life. And Alonzo also helped take care of the people who meant the most to him.

Despite his difficult childhood, Zo had mended fences with both his parents. He provides for both of them, and his father sometimes goes with him on road trips. He bought his father a home and also bought a home in a fine section of Chesapeake, Virginia, for Fannie Threet, his foster mom. There, she continues to help kids like Alonzo who need her. And wherever he goes, Zo always finds time to help kids like those at the Thompson Children's Home.

"Zo's a very sensitive person to other people and teammates," said his college coach, John Thompson. "Anyone who knows him will tell you that."

So Zo moved on to Miami for the 1995–1996 season. He was playing under a one-year contract and could be a free agent when the season ended. But some said that the Heat might want him to be their franchise center for many years.

"I expect to be here for the long haul," he told a reporter shortly after arriving in Miami. "But anything's capable of happening."

The Heat were also an expansion team that started play the same year as the Hornets. Miami, too, was looking to become a winner. That season the team had a new coach in Pat Riley, who had won several NBA titles with the Lakers and had then coached the New York Knicks to the finals two years earlier. The rugged Mourning was Riley's type of player.

"Alonzo is a whirling dervish, a cyclone of a player," said the coach. "He embodies everything we want this team to be—passionate, committed, aggressive, tireless. Those aren't vague concepts you have to try to get across to your players. You just say, 'Look at Zo.'"

Zo's work ethic didn't change at Miami. He still battled the NBA's best night after night. It was never easy playing the Bulls, especially when he had to go up against tough defensive star Dennis Rodman.

And Zo's work ethic never changed. Even after the rough practices that Riley ran, Zo would stay an extra two or three hours to work out on his own. Though he wanted to be very well paid for his services, Zo continued to work as hard as or harder than any player in the league.

The Heat didn't have a really deep team, though it did boast some fine players, like forward Billy Owens, guard Bimbo Coles, and power forward Kevin Willis. Now, as Pat Riley said, the team had its first-ever superstar.

Because he arrived in Miami just a day or two before the season began, Zo needed time to learn about his new team. He scored only 15 points in the opener, blocking 5 shots. He also made mistakes.

"I'm a little disappointed in the way I played," Zo said. "But it's going to come."

And it did. Against Orlando and Shaq on November 11, he scored 21 points and grabbed 12 boards. Against the Golden State Warriors on November 22, he had 27 points, 12 rebounds, and 8 blocks. Then in a game against the Dallas Mavericks on November 28, Zo hit on 16 of 21 field goals and 5 of 7 from the free-throw line for a season high 38 points. And the Heat were winning.

But, ever the competitor, Zo took the Miami fans to task. He didn't feel they were being vocal enough in support of the team. And he was always one to speak his mind.

"Maybe I'm kind of spoiled by Charlotte's fans," he said. "They generated so much energy for us, they used to get us up. A lot of fans here, when I see them sitting in the stands, they're laying back and relaxing. You know, we're out there, we're somewhat of a form of entertainment to them, but they've really got to get more into the game. If the fans are into it, we get into it. That gives us the extra incentive to work just as hard, not only for ourselves, but for them, too, because they're putting forth the effort and cheering for us."

Shortly afterward, Zo suffered a partially torn tendon in his foot that sidelined him for 12 games. Billy Owens was also hurt, as were several other players. Though Zo scored 38 in his first game back and continued to play at an All-Star level, the club still struggled. After an 11–3 start, the Heat had fallen to a 17–21 record by the third week in January. That meant that the team lost 18 of 24 games, including 9 of 12 while Zo was hurt.

"Man, what happened to our 11–3 start?" he asked, speaking for a lot of people. "We have to start from scratch. But you can [still] expect big things out of us."

In the second half of the season the team picked up former All-Star point guard Tim Hardaway from Golden State. With Zo healthy, the Heat finished strong, making the playoffs with a 42–40 record. They were the eighth and final team from the Eastern Conference to make it into the postseason.

Zo finished the regular season with a 23.2 average in 70 games. That tied with Charles Barkley for sixth place in the NBA scoring race. His 10.4 rebounding average was eighth best, but he was fifth in blocked

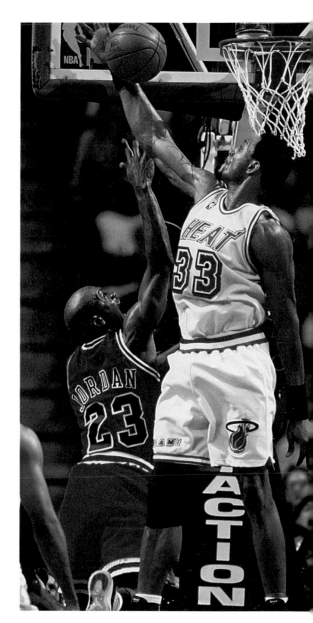

Looking almighty, Zo soars in the air to grab a rebound from Bulls superstar Michael Jordan.

shots with 2.7 per game. The problem was that the Heat would have to play the record-setting Chicago Bulls in the first round of the playoffs. The Bulls, led by Michael Jordan, were an amazing 72–10 in the regular season.

"We know we're capable of beating the Bulls," Zo said. "There's no big mystery about that. We've done it already this year."

But it wasn't to be. Chicago eliminated the Heat in three straight games and would go on to win the NBA championship. Zo and the rest of the Heat were disappointed. None of them had played well. But with Riley at the helm and Alonzo Mourning in the middle, Miami still felt hopeful for the future.

Alonzo Mourning continues to be a puzzle to some people. They see a ferocious player who never smiles on the basketball court. They see an athlete who turned down a $78-million contract to force a trade because he felt he was worth more. And he got more, signing a long-term contract with Miami after the season ended. It was said to be worth around $100 million.

What the public doesn't always see, however, is the human being who loves talking with small children and trying to improve the quality of their lives. They don't see an intelligent college graduate who has purchased homes for his father and for the woman who raised him. They don't always see an athlete who plays his heart out every night and wants nothing more than for his team to win.

All of that is Alonzo Mourning, one of the hardest-working and best athletes of our time.

Despite playing his heart out as usual, Zo and his Miami teammates were eliminated from the 1996 playoffs by the Bulls.

ALONZO MOURNING: HIGHLIGHTS

1970   Born on February 8 in Chesapeake, Virginia.

1984   Enters Indian River High School.

1987   In his junior year, leads Indian River High School to an unbeaten record and the state championship.
Named Virginia's High School Player of the Year.

1988   Named National High School Player of the Year by Gatorade and *USA Today*.
Enters Georgetown University.

1989   Sets a Georgetown single-season record and leads the nation with 169 blocks.
Named 1988–1989 Big East Defensive Player of the Year.
Named to 1988–1989 Second Team All-Big East.
Named to 1988–1989 Big East All-Rookie Team.

1990   Named Big East Co-Defensive Player of the Year.
Named to 1989–1990 First Team All-Big East.

1992   Named First Team All-American by Associated Press.
Named Big East Defensive Player of the Year.
Named Eastern Basketball Player of the Year.
Wins Henry Iba Defensive Player of the Year Award
Drafted by Charlotte Hornets (1st round, 2nd pick overall) in NBA draft.

1993   Blocks 271 shots during his rookie season—fourth best in the NBA.

1994   Leads Hornets in scoring (21.5 points per game average), rebounding (10.2 per game), and blocks (3.13 per game).

1995   Leads Hornets in scoring (21.3 points per game average), rebounding (9.9 per game), blocks (2.92 per game), and field goal percentage (.519).
Is traded to the Miami Heat for forward Glen Rice just before the start of the 1995–1996 season.

1996   Leads Heat into playoffs, averaging 23.2 points per game.
Signs long-term contract to remain in Miami.

FIND OUT MORE

Brooks, Philip. *Dikembe Mutombo: Mount Mutombo.* Danbury, CT: Childrens Press, 1995.

Cohen, Neil. *Head to Head Basketball: Patrick Ewing and Alonzo Mourning.* New York: Bantam, 1994.

Gutman, Bill. *Basketball.* North Bellmore, NY: Marshall Cavendish, 1990.

Knapp, Ron. *Top Ten Basketball Centers.* Springfield, NJ: Enslow Publishers, 1994.

Weber, Bruce. *Pro Basketball Megastars.* New York: Scholastic, 1995.

How to write to Alonzo Mourning:
Alonzo Mourning
c/o Miami Heat
Miami Arena
Miami, FL 33136

INDEX